The ARCHITECTS

William Penn's cottage, Letitia Court, Philadelphia, Pennsylvania, built about 1683, (Historical Society of Pennsylvania)

COLONIAL AMERICANS

The ARCHITECTS

WRITTEN & ILLUSTRATED BY

Leonard Everett Fisher

WITH ADDITIONAL PHOTOGRAPHS

FRANKLIN WATTS, INC.
575 Lexington Avenue, New York, N.Y. 10022

For my brother,
Richard Arnold Fisher,
architect, civil engineer

SBN 531 1041-4

Library of Congress Catalog Card Number: 70-101748

Printed in the United States of America

1 2 3 4 5

Colonial Americans

THE ARCHITECTS
THE CABINETMAKERS
THE DOCTORS
THE GLASSMAKERS
THE HATTERS
THE LIMNERS
THE PAPERMAKERS
THE PEDDLERS
THE POTTERS
THE PRINTERS
THE SCHOOLMASTERS
THE SHOEMAKERS
THE SILVERSMITHS
THE TANNERS
THE WEAVERS
THE WIGMAKERS

Constructing the fort at Jamestown, Virginia.

The Southern Colonies

A hazy morning sun warmed the quiet Virginia land above the mouth of the James River. There, three small ships — the *Susan Constant*, the *Discovery*, and the *Goodspeed* — moored to the river trees the night before, rolled lazily in the water. Their 145 passengers and crewmen had completed a four-months' crossing of the Atlantic, westward from England. Now the voyagers crowded the rails and rigging and looked at the green American wilderness.

Before the sun had risen much higher in the sky, they would leave the ships and begin to erect a fort and some buildings. By the end of that day, May 14, 1607, the first permanent English settlement, Jamestown, would be rooted in the soil of North America.

Among those first colonists there was no one whose job it was to help the builders by making a plan of the fort beforehand. Today, over three hundred years later, this would be the work of an architect. An architect has had careful training in building construction and design. He must be able to plan a building that is suitable for its uses. He must understand building materials and the various methods of construction, so that his structure will be strong and will not collapse. His building must be pleasing to look at, with good proportions and with all its parts in harmony. And he must think it out and put all its details and measurements into working drawings before construction even starts. The builders follow his plans.

No one among the Jamestown voyagers had been trained in this work. There was no recognized profession of architecture in Great Britain during most of the seventeenth century. There were no architectural schools. Most of the English structures of that time were planned either by the people who wanted them built, or they were designed by the man who did the actual building: the master builder, trained to supervise other workers; the housewright, or house builder; or the plain carpenter.

Not even Christopher Wren, the man who designed so many of the great buildings of London after the disastrous fire of 1666, was a trained architect as we understand such a profession today. Wren was a mathematician, an astronomer, and the royal surveyor for Charles II. In architecture, he was self-taught.

Nevertheless, Wren seems to have had the basic skills necessary to do outstanding work. He had a fine knowledge of the construction, purposes, and appearance of various types of buildings. He knew a great deal about architectural styles such as those of classical Greece and Rome or the more recent Renaissance Italy, France, and Flanders. He had ideas of his own, a sense of order, and a feeling for symmetry. He knew how to use brick, stone, or wood — the chief building materials of the day — in a manner that was similar to continental European styles, yet was distinctively English.

Before Wren, another Englishman, Inigo Jones, had become interested in architecture. He was appointed royal surveyor to James I in 1615. Jones had traveled widely in Italy and had

Front of building and room plan from Architecture, Book II, by Andrea Palladio. (New York Public Library)

studied the buildings of a sixteenth-century Italian architect, Andrea Palladio. Palladio had examined the architectural styles of ancient Rome and had used their elements in designing his own buildings. His use of arches, columns, windows, and the like was later called Palladian.

With certain variations, Jones introduced Palladio's Renaissance version of classical Roman architecture into an England whose buildings at that time largely followed the style of medieval days. In so doing, he set English architecture on a new course that continued, with more variations, through Christopher Wren and others. Many of the skilled English builders learned to use some of Wren's and Jones's ideas in their own structures. And in time, American builders, too, were influenced by these ideas.

But in 1607, the crude, thatch-roofed structures at Jamestown were designed and built by untrained men, not architects. These men were interested in quick protection from hostile Indians and bad weather, not in the creation of beautiful buildings. Perhaps it can be said that they were the first British architect-builders in

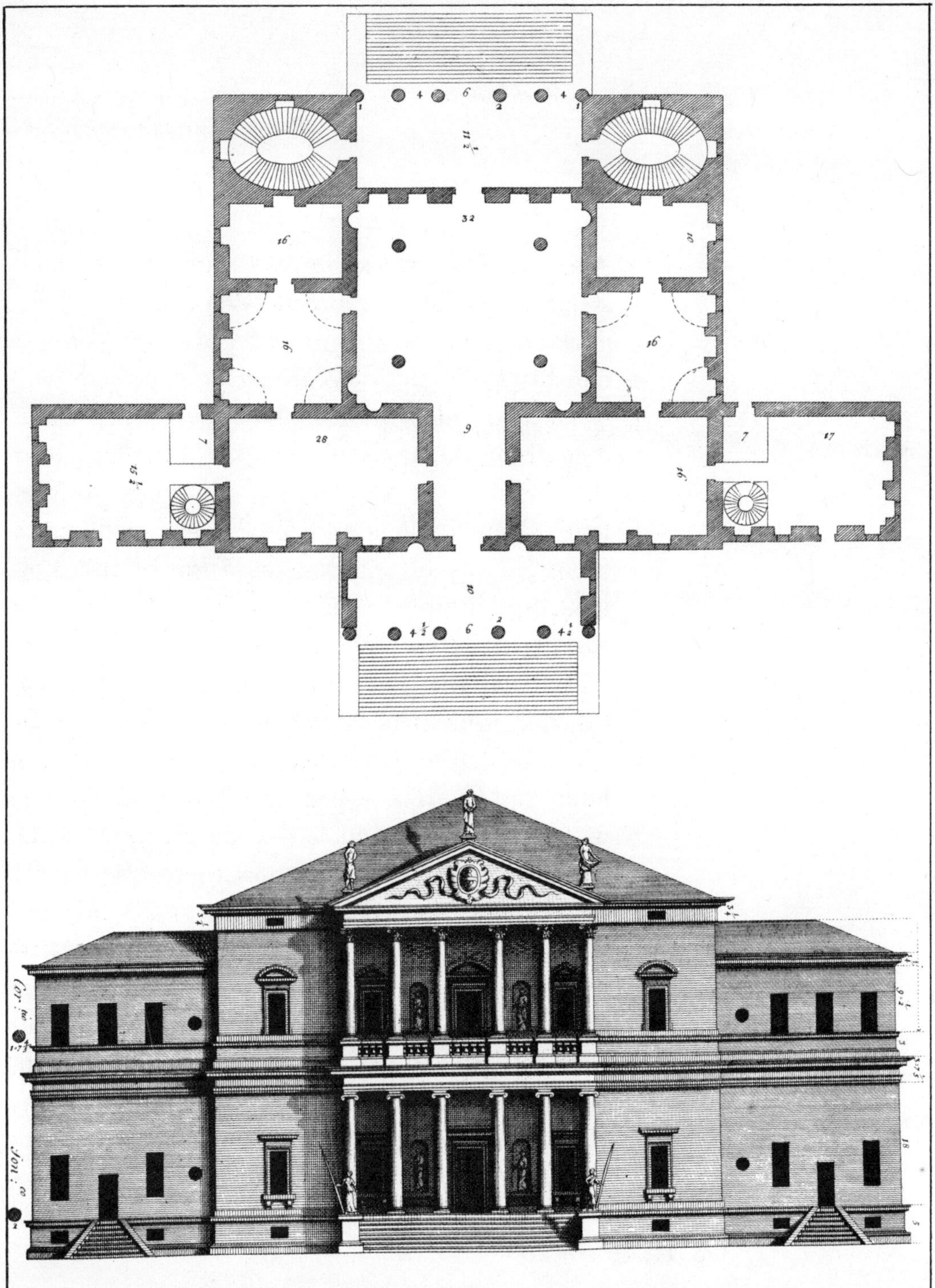

Early houses in Jamestown were like the rough country dwellings of England at that time.

America. Their work crew was made up of about a dozen unskilled laborers, several boys, a half-dozen carpenters, two or three bricklayers without bricks or a brickyard, a stonemason, and some assorted helpers, chiefly the common seamen from the ships' crews. The rough shelters they made were like similar structures in England. These workers were Englishmen, who knew no other way of building than that of the common dwelling places they had left behind in the rural parts of the homeland.

As time went on, other colonies were established in the southeastern region of North America. The southern colonies — Virginia, the Carolinas, and Georgia — became plantation country, with landowners who had huge estates. In the eastern part of these colonies there was hardly any middle class at all. True, small farmers, shopkeepers, innkeepers, tavernkeepers, craftsmen, clergymen, and the like were scattered in the widely separated towns and villages. But they were economically dependent on the plantation crops of tobacco, rice, and indigo. In the main, only two classes made up colonial south-

LEF

Many builders took their ideas from books on architecture.

ern society. There were the rich or near-rich planters, and there were all the people — indentured servants, craftsmen, and black slaves — who depended on the planters' success or failure. Only the rich planters and the royal governors of the colonies could afford to put their architectural ideas to work for them. Only in public buildings, plantation mansions, and elegant town houses was there formal planning on any scale at all.

By the early years of the eighteenth century some men with architectural training were coming to America from England. They brought with them a thorough knowledge of the new architectural practices. Besides these men, many workmen skilled in the building trades had immigrated, too. They had solid experience in working on many kinds of structures, and they too were alert to new architectural ways.

But perhaps most important of all were the books these men brought with them. In England at this time there was a tremendous interest in architecture. Many manuals and books on the subject were being published, and they were

LEF

Details for a fireplace, from Batty Langley's Treasury of Designs.
(New York Public Library)

available to everyone. Some of these books dealt with architectural styles; some showed actual building designs and plans; some were practical manuals on the building crafts; some were combinations of these things.

Among them were Andrea Palladio's books; *The City and Country Purchaser and Builder,* by Stephen Primatt; *The Art of House Carpentry,* by Joseph Moxon; *The Modern Builder's Assistant,* by William Halfpenny; and works showing the designs of Inigo Jones, Christopher Wren, and lesser building planners. One book, perhaps used most of all, was *The City and Country Builder's and Workman's Treasury of Designs*, by Batty Langley. It had hundreds of detailed drawings of every part of a house. Another much-used volume was *A Book of Architecture*, by James Gibbs, an English architect. He wrote the book hoping, as he said, that it might be of help to "such gentlemen as might be concerned in building, especially in the remote parts of the country, where little or no assistance for design can be procured."

The Measures Invented proportioned and affixed by Batty Langley 1730.

Phototypie Paul & Vigier - Paris

40 — From LANGLEY — Treasury of Designs

Everyone, builders and architects alike, used these books, and borrowed the details they wanted to put into their own structures. In many instances the planter who was paying for the house became his own architect, although he was only an amateur. At that time, almost every educated gentleman had some knowledge of architecture, and every gentleman could sketch at least a little. Many of the planters had visited England and had seen English architecture. Their own ideas, added to the ideas in the books, might see them through, when it came to planning a house.

The design of a home depended on how well a planter could understand architectural books and the principles of architecture and how well he could select and adapt what was useful for his own needs. And it depended on the craftsmen he hired, their knowledge of building, and their ability to carry out their employer's ideas. Together, the planter and the builder often laid out rough plans for the house. Finished working drawings such as are used today were unknown. Decorative details were often copied from books. It is even possible today to compare drawings in certain of the old books with certain still existing colonial houses, and to find the resemblances between them.

Usually the planter or the royal governor hired a master builder to supervise the actual construction. The builder had been trained in a long apprenticeship and by long experience and had a thorough knowledge of the practical and technical details of construction. He was skilled at the necessary crafts and he understood how to use the needed materials. His standard of workmanship was high.

Often as not, English master builders were sent for. When these men arrived in the southern colonies they found that there were not enough good craftsmen to do the work at hand, partly because the southern colonies were thinly populated. The master builder would have to find one or two craftsmen — a carpenter, a bricklayer-mason — who could teach some of the plantation slaves the housewright crafts. Or perhaps the master craftsman himself would teach them. In many instances, the black Africans proved to be superior to the white men who taught them.

Carter's Grove plantation house, Williamsburg, Virginia, built 1750–55. (Colonial Williamsburg photograph)

Typical of the wealthy, privileged southern planter and his master builder was Carter Burwell, landowner. Burwell's 300,000-acre plantation, Carter's Grove, was a few miles east of Jamestown. In 1750 he hired several housewrights, among them David Minitree and John Wheatley, to construct an up-to-date English country home at Carter's Grove. The mansion was to be in the popular Georgian style of the day. The housewrights employed whatever carpenters, bricklayers, and masons they could find in and around Williamsburg, the Virginia capital. In addition, they instructed a number of slaves in their particular skills. Carter Burwell also brought from England a remarkable woodworking craftsman, Richard Baylis, who did the interior paneling of the house. The actual design was probably the work of Richard Taliaferro, who planned some other houses of the time.

The Georgian style of architecture had been gradually developed under the reigns of the first three Georges, kings of England. The usual Georgian house was a formal, well-balanced rectangle, at least two stories high and built around

Governor's Palace, Williamsburg, Virginia, built 1710–20.
(Colonial Williamsburg photo)

a central hall or stairway. The windows were evenly spaced all around the building. Chimneys rose from both ends of the structure. Whatever ornament appeared, inside and out, was usually of wood and was based on classical designs.

Another master builder, Henry Cary, was hired by the royal governor of Virginia, Alexander Spotswood, to supervise the construction of the governor's palace at Williamsburg. Cary had previously been responsible for the building of Williamsburg's capitol building. Spotswood himself was an excellent mathematician, and familiar with architectural design. His handsome brick residence, begun in 1710, took ten years to complete. The governor not only contributed much advice on the design, but personally supervised some of the building. In 1715, he designed Williamsburg's eight-sided brick magazine for the storage of arms and ammunition.

In 1765, John Hawks, an English architect, was hired by Governor William Tryon of North Carolina to design and supervise the construction of the governor's palace in that colony. Not long after, in 1767, a gifted amateur architect,

Thomas Jefferson's home, Monticello, with floor plan. (Jefferson Memorial Foundation)

twenty-four-year-old Thomas Jefferson, began to design Monticello, his future home near Charlottesville, Virginia. Jefferson had read all the available architectural handbooks and had taught himself how to make working drawings. Like many English aristocrats, he favored the ideas of Andrea Palladio, the Italian architect. He incorporated many of them into his own design. English buildings, however, had been designed in the Palladian style for at least one hundred years before Jefferson's time, and this style had appeared in the Virginia countryside some years before the future American President turned his lively mind to architecture.

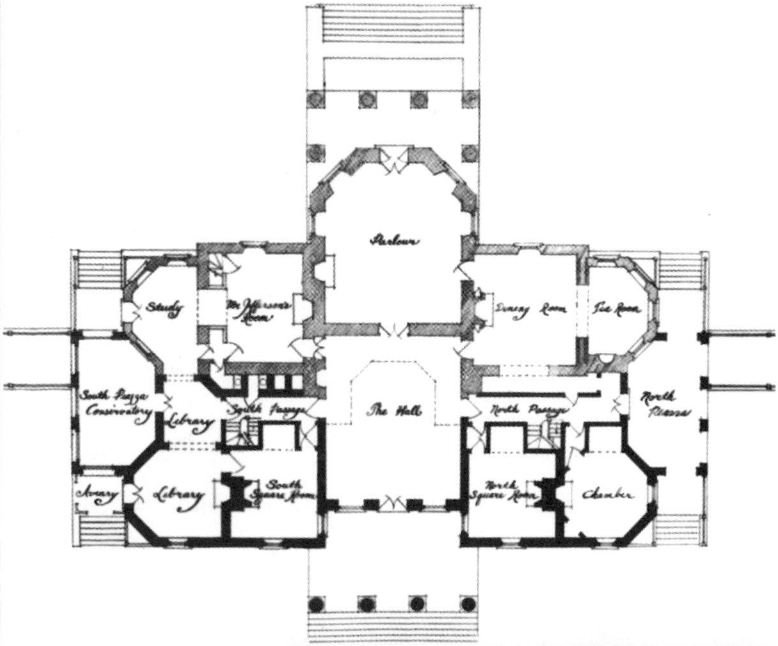
Parlour
Study
Mr Jefferson's Room
Dining Room
Tea Room
South Piazza Conservatory
Library
South Passage
The Hall
North Passage
North Piazza
Aviary
Library
South Square Room
North Square Room
Chamber

Pilgrims building a house in Plymouth.

The New England Colonies

Thirteen years after Jamestown was established, another band of English voyagers — the Pilgrim Separatists — stumbled up a desolate slope above a Massachusetts beach. On this spot, which they called Plymouth, they decided to build their fort and houses.

There were no architects among this group of farmers and craftsmen. The nearest thing to a housebuilder was the ship's carpenter. Another man with some knowledge of woodwork was John Alden, twenty-one, a ship's cooper, or barrelmaker, who had been hired by the Pilgrims to watch over their precious casks of drinking water during the voyage. Alden had decided to remain with the Pilgrims. He soon learned the carpentry skills needed for building the crude shelters at Plymouth.

Most of the Pilgrims and other early settlers in New England had to rely on themselves when it came to building their houses and meetinghouse-churches. But a few of the wealthy leaders, Governor John Winthrop of the Massachusetts Bay Colony among them, could have others do the work for them. Between 1630 and 1649, Governor Winthrop had the colony carpenters build at least three houses for him — in Charlestown, Cambridge, and Newtown, now Newton.

In 1638, another leader, Samuel Symonds, wrote a letter to the son of the governor. In it he described in every construction detail the two-and-one-half story house he wanted built for himself in Ipswich. "Be sure," he wrote, among other things, "that all the doorways in every place be so high that any man may go upright under."

In all likelihood the man who supervised the construction of these homes was the colony's chief all-around artisan, Thomas Graves. It was Graves who, by order of the Massachusetts Bay Colony, built a large meetinghouse in Charlestown in 1629 — a full year before enough people would arrive to use it.

In the beginning, the New Englanders built simple structures of thatch, rough timbers, and wattle—a lacework of twigs mixed with mud, straw, and clay. In most respects these crude buildings were no different from the thatch-roofed medieval cottages that dotted the English countryside and in which most of the settlers had lived at one time or another. The new houses in America were constructed rapidly, to provide shelter as soon as possible. They hardly required the special skills of a trained architect, as the colonists were thoroughly familiar with the simple building plan.

Before long, however, the colonists began to build all-wood frame houses. These were somewhat larger than their earlier cottages, and better suited to the extremes of New England weather.

Many of the newer houses were built by Puritan carpenters for a rapidly growing middle class. In 1640, a weaver, William Rix, hired John Davys, a carpenter, to build him a one-and-one-half story clapboard house. Like most housewrights of the time, Davys was unschooled in architecture. The man who hired him merely told him the size of the house he wanted, how many rooms it should have, and any other neces-

The old John Ward house in Salem, Massachusetts, built in 1684, has the high roof line and overhanging upper story of a medieval house.
(Essex Institute, Salem, Massachusetts)

sary details, and Davys, an experienced man, built it.

Neither Davys nor the New England wilderness was ready for elaborate house designs. The colonists could hardly afford luxury, and furthermore they did not want it. They were simple people whose basic religious beliefs led them to plain ways of living. They preferred the traditions they were used to. With some small differences they continued in the New World the fundamentally medieval look of the England they had left behind.

During most of the seventeenth century, New England housewrights and carpenters kept the high, angular roof lines and overhanging upper stories of medieval houses. What small changes were made were brought about chiefly by the new American environment, with its unpredictable climate. And though the Puritans did not seek an artistic effect, their simply styled structures had a quiet, orderly beauty when set in the rugged, rolling New England countryside.

By the end of the seventeenth century a gradual shift was taking place in the architecture of

A New England bricklayer, turned master builder, supervises his workmen.

New England. No longer was New England solely Puritan. Now there was a variety of nationalities and religions. The middle class was becoming prosperous. Many people were no longer content to live in simple workaday houses. They had created new and substantial lives for themselves. The more wealthy among them wanted fashionable homes and public buildings that would reflect their new position in the world.

The architectural styles of Jones and Wren, and through them the styles of the earlier Palladio, were becoming widely known in New England at about the same time as in the southern colonies. New England gentlemen, like gentlemen in the south, were becoming avid readers of architectural handbooks and how-to-do-it manuals. So too were the New England carpenters, bricklayers, masons, and woodworkers.

But unlike the southern colonies, New England was more heavily populated and had no shortage of skilled workmen. The northern craftsmen who were trained in the old tradition, and the fashionably modern architectural enthusiasts who hired them, together produced an extraordi-

LEF

Interior view of Touro Synagogue, Newport, Rhode Island, built in 1762. (Library of Congress)

nary number of buildings that were handsome in their simplicity and quiet ornament. Most of these buildings were not altogether original, as they had been designed by people who borrowed their ideas from the architectural manuals. But the builder-architects put together the details with great harmony and created buildings that were not quite English, but very New England — sturdy, orderly, unpretentious, and dignified.

Outstanding among the eighteenth-century New England gentlemen-architects was Peter Harrison (1716–1775) of Newport, Rhode Island. He was a merchant, a farmer, and a ship-handler, and he owned one of the best and largest libraries of architectural books in America. Drawing freely on the designs of Palladio, Jones, Gibbs, and Wren, Harrison created a number of buildings that attracted attention. These buildings included the second King's Chapel in Boston, and the Brick Market and the Touro Synagogue, both in Newport.

Boston's red-brick Christ Church Episcopal, or Old North Church, is a further present-day example of outstanding architecture from the

colonial period. Ebenezer Clough and James Varney built the Old North Church, begun in 1723. The architect is believed to have been a Boston engraver, William Price. Price had been to London, where he had studied the architecture of London churches, some fifty of which were designed by Christopher Wren. Price designed the spire under which, on the night of April 18, 1775, two lanterns were lit to warn patriots in Charlestown that the British were crossing the river on their way to Concord and the first skirmish of the American Revolution.

Steeple of Old North Church, Boston, Massachusetts—building started in 1723. (Library of Congress)

LEF

A house built in the typical stepped-roof Dutch style of the early 1700's.

The Middle Atlantic Colonies

The long, irregular seaboard marking the eastern edge of New York, New Jersey, and Pennsylvania had been explored long before Jamestown and Plymouth became permanent English outposts on the North American continent. It was not until 1609, however, that Henry Hudson, an Englishman employed by the Dutch, claimed these middle regions for the Netherlands.

Not many years after Hudson's explorations, Dutch fur traders were flourishing throughout the area. Some permanent Dutch settlements were built — Fort Orange, now Albany, New York; and Fort Amsterdam, on the tip of Manhattan Island, now New York City.

From the very beginning of their colonization in America the Hollanders had engaged in brisk business with the Indian trappers. Most of the Dutch were so busy trading that they failed to establish strong, well-knit communities. The wealthy among them carved out huge estates for themselves, mostly in the Hudson River Valley, leaving little opportunity for others.

Some Swedish colonists tried to settle in New Jersey and Pennsylvania, along the Delaware River. For seventeen years, between 1638 and 1655, they fought to subdue the wilderness and establish themselves in that area. But in the end the Dutch sent a military expedition against them and captured the colony for Holland. Nonetheless, the Swedes managed to introduce a non-English type of building to America: the log cabin. From this time on, American frontiersmen became their own architects, building simple log cabins as they pushed westward through the forests.

Unlike the southern and New England colonies, which were British in character during the entire colonial period, the Middle Atlantic colonies were a mixture of numerous nationalities — Swedish, Dutch, French, English, German, and others. All during the seventeenth century each individual national group raised buildings that resembled those in its homeland.

The familiar thatch-roofed medieval English cottages appeared in the Middle Atlantic colonies only to be replaced quickly by clapboard houses with steep, sloping roofs. They, in turn, gave way to small red-brick houses. The Dutch built their traditional brick houses with stepped gable roofs as early as 1628. Some of the brick was imported from Holland, but a good deal of it was made by the Rensselaer family near Albany. All the various national groups used nearly the same local materials for building: timber, stone, clay, slate, brick, straw, tile.

Here, during the seventeenth century — as elsewhere along the Atlantic coast — there were no architects and few how-to-do-it manuals. The people designed and built their own houses or hired carpenters, bricklayers, or masons to do the work for them. The English, Dutch, Swedish, German, or French flavor of these buildings was the result of the background of the builder.

In the eighteenth century, more and more Englishmen arrived in New York, New Jersey, and Pennsylvania, and the same change in architectural design that was occurring in New Eng-

Independence Hall, Philadelphia, Pennsylvania, built 1732–50. (National Park Service)

land took place in the Middle Atlantic colonies. Not only was the medieval look disappearing, but the national groups who had once laid claim to parts of the area were taking on the ways of the English.

Christopher Wren and Inigo Jones and the new Georgian style were as fashionable in prosperous Philadelphia as they were in Boston or the southern colonies, especially in the design of public buildings. Architectural handbooks became readily available to people in the Middle Colonies. Good, hardworking craftsmen were plentiful. And again, a small group of master carpenters and amateur gentleman-architects created some outstanding buildings.

Among these men were two Philadelphians, Edmund Woolley, master carpenter, and Andrew Hamilton, lawyer. Borrowing freely from the English manuals, these men designed and supervised the construction of one of the handsomest buildings in all America — the Pennsylvania State House, later renamed Independence Hall. Begun in 1732 and completed about 1750, it was a fine example of Georgian design.

BARRY

Woolley later joined with three other master builders — Samuel Rhoads, David Evans, and Robert Smith — to design and build a structure where their guild, the Carpenters' Company of Philadelphia, could meet. The guild itself was founded in 1724 for a variety of reasons, some professional, some charitable. But the basic reason was "to obtain instruction in the science of

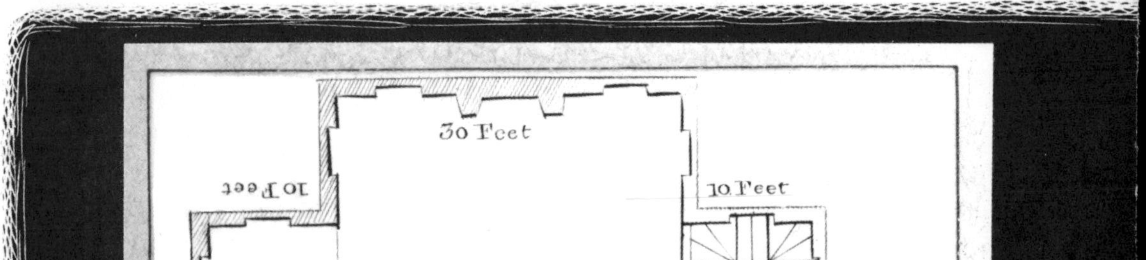

Original floor plan, Carpenters' Hall, Philadelphia, Pennsylvania, built 1770–74. (National Park Service)

Carpenters' Hall, Philadelphia, Pennsylvania—
front of hall as originally built.
(National Park Service)

architecture." This guild was the first organization of architect-builders in America.

In 1770, ground was broken for Carpenters' Hall. Four years later, in 1774, the unusual cross-shaped Georgian building was completed. In September of that same year, Carpenters' Hall became the meeting place of the First Continental Congress.

The colonial period did not end until seven years later, when Great Britain finally surrendered the thirteen colonies. Yet, in some ways, the meeting of the Continental Congress, to protest Britain's earlier actions, was the beginning of the end of the colonial era in America.

The carpenters of Philadelphia had no way of knowing in 1770 for what purposes, other than their own, Carpenters' Hall might be used. But somehow it was fitting that men like these, who designed and built things for a living and for the comfort and pleasure of others, should have provided a meeting place for a different group of "architects" — the men who laid the first foundations of a new nation, the United States of America.

Index